CHINESE PHILOSOPHY ON LIFE

Wang Keping

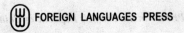

FOREIGN LANGUAGES PRESS

First Edition 2005
Second Printing 2007

ISBN 978-7-119-04179-7
©Foreign Languages Press, Beijing, China, 2005

Published by Foreign Languages Press
24 Baiwanzhuang Road, Beijing 100037, China
Website: http://www.flp.com.cn
E-mail Addresses: Info@flp.com.cn
Sales@flp.com.cn

Distributed by China International Book Trading Corporation
35 Chegongzhuang Xilu, Beijing 100044, China
P.O.Box 399, Beijing, China

Printed in the People's Republic of China

Preface

Heracleitus argues that one cannot step into the same river twice. This is due to his hypothesis that everything is in an eternal flux or change. Metaphorically speaking, all is subject to this "eternal flux" to the extent that the moment one steps into "the river" once again, the flowing water, time, space, location and even the person himself are no longer the same as they used to be. Such is the dramatic consequence disregarding that an idiosyncratic self may still imagine the possibility of repeating an action with sameness.

Quite the reverse, I have a fancy to say that if one confronts with a river of value systems, he or she may step into it more than twice. This does not mean that the value systems themselves are exempt from any kind of change or modification. It means that the process of change in this case is always bearing a historical continuity and present-day relevance, so to speak. Such continuity and relevance are not merely embodied in the fact that we are making and living in the history at the same time, but also in the tendency that we read new ideas and messages into the old texts including value systems as primary components within.

Part of the value systems are originated and formulated in the ancient Chinese classics. These classics as old texts are read and reread as timeless ones all along in the history. Right in the digital age against the context of economic and cultural globalization today, we human beings alike seem to be falling into a paradoxical situation. On the one hand we tend to advantage ourselves in a material or technical sense, and therefore enjoy

more conveniences and comforts; but on the other, we tend to disadvantage ourselves in a spiritual sense as we are frequently haunted by such negative experience as pressure, frustration, anxiety, failure, and meaninglessness, etc. Coincidently or not, we return to the ancient philosophy on human existence in order to rediscover a relevance of values and a sense of homeness. This happens to help revive the Chinese philosophy on life in general, even conducing to the thought that philosophy therapy can perform a necessary but different function if compared with psychological therapy.

It is noteworthy that the term "philosophy" (*philosophia*) is here used in a conventionally Hellenic sense. It implies "the love of wisdom" (*philocum-sophia*). "Wisdom" as *sophia* carries a two-fold implication. It is relating to both theory (*theoria*) and praxis (*praxis*). Theory in this regard involves contemplation and reflection through mind, whereas praxis involves doing and taking action via body. This being the case, "philosophy" is cor-

responding to "wisdom" with a type of "love" to reinforce the theoretical and practical dimensions and their dynamic synthesis as well. According to this logic, "philosophy on life" as is sketched subsequently in this book is expected to stir up theoretical thinking and practical doing all together because they are equally important.

I hereby take this occasion to extend my sincere thanks to Miss Li Xia, deputy editor-in-chief of *China Today*, for her initiative to open up a special feature in the journal and her encouraging me to contribute these rambling short essays for general readers. Without her kind advice, I must confess, I would have attended to something else instead of writing these conversational pieces. Meanwhile, I highly appreciate what Mr. Hu Kaimin has done to bring this book into such shape. Once again I acknowledge my heartfelt thanks to Miss Lu Shuang as her artistic and philosophical illustrations make the verbal expositions more enlightening and significant.

Finally, I sincerely hope that our dear readers might find it worthwhile when time is so pressing nowadays.

Wang Keping
Early spring, 2005

CONTENTS

CONTENTS

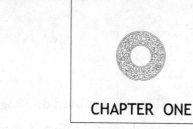

CHAPTER ONE

The Interplay between fortune and misfortune

Time and the seasons in China's countryside pass according to the agricultural Lunar Calendar, and at least one festival is celebrated each month. Most important is Spring Festival (*chunjie*), when whole families reunite to celebrate the transition from winter to spring. At this time the indoor walls

"Fu Dao"

of all freshly scrubbed dwellings are decorated with papercuts and works of calligraphy representing the Chinese character *fu*, generally on red paper. This character is often seen upside down on household doors, screens, and walls, signifying *"fu dao"* — the arrival of *fu*.

So, what does this all-important *fu* mean? Good fortune, naturally, which generally brings with it happiness. This is the character's overall meaning. It derives from the pictogram below(Fig.1), which symbolizes a figure kneeling and praying for happiness before an altar, on which is placed a gourd shaped container of valuables, as a wisp of smoke from burning incense wafts upward. This was the basis for the *zhuan* style *fu* (Fig.2), but the character has since been simplified to its present

Fig.1 *The "Fu" character is derived from this pictogram.*

form (Fig.3). The left-hand component symbolizes the altar, and that on the right a jewel box. The complete character therefore represents a combined aspiration towards both spiritual and material well being. The common belief is that as long as a person or family retains *fu*, their life will be happy and fulfilled.

Fig.2 福   Fig.3 福   Fig.4 祸   Fig.5 祸

The antithesis of *fu* is *huo*, in *zhuan* style written as Fig.4 and in simplified form as Fig.5. Components of the character *huo* are, again, an altar to the left, but on the right is a picture of a crooked mouth — a harbinger of misfortune or harm to be avoided at all costs. The Chinese use *huo* (ill fortune or calamity) as a generic term for all things negative or destructive, to the extent that a *huogen* (祸根) is a person or thing that brings misfortune to the majority.

3

In China, as everywhere, *fu* is widely sought after, while *huo* is avoided at all costs. As a topic of conversation, *fu* is one fulsomely expanded, extended and lingered upon, while *huo* is only mentioned when absolutely necessary, and never dwelt upon. Should the subject of *huo* come up too frequently in a person's daily life and social interactions,

祸

they might begin to feel nervous or apprehensive, or even offended. The Chinese people are nonetheless fully aware of the interplay between *fu* and *huo*, partly through the basic Daoist *Yin* (negative)/*Yang* (positive) principle, but mostly through their insight, born of experience, into the human condition. They are aware that *fu* and *huo* occur in parallel to life's ups and downs and joys and griefs. This is clear from everyday Chinese proverbs, such as *le ji sheng bei*, "extreme joy begets sorrow," and *ku jin gan lai*, "Bitter experience may turn

福

4

to sweet joy."The former refers to positive changing to negative and the reverse is true of the latter. Hence, at times of euphoria born of an unexpected blessing a Chinese person is instinctively aware that, having reached a pinnacle, it would be all too easy to make a sudden descent into misery .They therefore do their best to keep their emotions in check. If, on the other hand, a person finds themselves in a woeful plight, they try not to lose hope, and to remain optimistic as they actively prusue a positive outcome. Western philosopher Bertrand Russell, who lived in China during the 1940s, was particularly impressed by what he perceived as "Oriental philosophical wisdom," as regards a Chinese person's capacity to extract pleasure from the meanest of situations, in the midst of poverty, privation and disaster. This still holds true today, and is no less impressive now than ever.

The Chinese apply *fu/huo* polarity to their temporal as well as spiritual life, their philosophical approach stemming largely from the teachings of Lao Zi, originator of the Taoism. Lao Zi was an older contemporary of Confucius, and so was at large during 500 BC. His observation of the interaction between fortune and misfortune is clear in his *Tao-Te Ching* when he says:

"Ill fortune is that beside which good fortune lies;

Good fortune is that beneath which all fortune lurks. "

This concept is also the theme of an ancient story:

There lived an old man near China's northern borders. When his horse wandered away into north-

ern tribe territory, his neighbors commiserated with him over his loss. "Perhaps this will turn out to be a blessing, " said the old man. After a few months, the horse came back accompanied by a mare from the north. Seeing this, all his neighbors congratulated him. "This could turn into misfortune," was the old man's comment. The mare

bore many fine horses, and he prospered for a time, until one day his son fell from a horse and broke his leg. The neighbors gathered around, and once more commiserated with the family, as the old man thought inwardly, "This could be a blessing." One year later, the northern tribes invaded the border regions, and all able-bodied young men were conscripted to fight the invaders. The old man's son, however, was exempt from fighting because of his crippled leg, and the two consequently survived the slaughter that followed.

This story comes from the Chinese classic, *Huainan Zi* and is familiar to all Chinese people. Its moral is that *huo* (disaster) is often *fu*(blessing) in disguise, and vice versa. Fortune and misfortune are opposite arcs of an interactive or transformational circle. The principle advocated is that it is advisable to look beyond what appears to be a positive event and stay alert in preparation for any possible negative "after shock." Within this concept, it is wise not to act rashly, but to exercise self-control over one's emotions. In this way a happy event is less likely to descend into misery. Such self-control calls for awareness of the *Dao* tenet, "*Reversal is when Dao moves,*" and the knowledge that the positive and negative are intertwined and culminate in *wu ji bi fan*, or "inevitable reversal of the extreme."

There is a belief among Chinese people that, philosophically speaking, the *Dao* moves along a dynamic, circular path, and that all things determined by *Dao* are part of a constantly changing process. There can be no control over opposites transforming into their antitheses other than by one who has achieved *Dao*, or complete enlightenment. Only then do fortune and misfortune remain in their original state of indistinguishable unity.

Lao Zi regarded the interplay between *fu* and *huo* and their reversals as an attendant aspect of reality. This could be interpreted as encouraging passivism and curbing initiative, because it suggests an inevitability of events that nullifies all human endeavor. In practice, however, fortune and misfortune change place only under particular circumstances. In the normal course of

events, they stay as they are, and unenlightened mortals can maintain the status quo by encouraging positive, rather than negative, interplay between good and bad fortune as they occur in everyday life.

CHAPTER TWO

The Soup Allegory of Harmony

Host and guests sit around a soup pot in the painting Feast and Festivity, from the Wei and Jin periods (220-420).

Whether a person eats to live or vice versa, everyone needs food. History bears witness to humankind's concept of food as a prerequisite for survival, the fulfillment of which also brings enor-

Chinese Philosophy on Life

mous sensual pleasure. Speaking as a Chinese person, enjoyment of food in all its colors, styles, tastes — even the symbolic names given to dishes based on the cooking expertise and the materials used, is part of my psyche. My experience and observations have given rise to the theory that Chinese wisdom has practical associations with Chinese dining etiquette.

When dining out in China at restaurants where local people go, it becomes clear immediately that

A whole-family feast is still an integral part of Chinese festival celebrations.(Photos by Shi Li)

12

the dishes placed on the table are not specifically for those who have ordered them, but are to be shared. On a fresh dish being served, the host or hostess picks out the choicest morsels for their guests, who reciprocate. A dinner generally begins with a warm-up period, when small talk, courtesies and toasts are exchanged. Things then liven up. Table conversation becomes animated, with much joking and laughing. The whole scene takes on a more familial ambience until a moment of supreme harmony is reached when discord born of class difference, personal prejudice, or the generation gap momentarily dissolves, and a feeling of shared warmth prevails. All present feel cheered and secure within the ethos of harmony — *he*.

The concept of harmony is the keystone within the Chinese philosophy of life. It is sought and nurtured in all occupations and pursuits, most particularly human relations. Harmony is advocated in Confucianism as a strategy through which to address social problems

and maintain an even social keel, as it stabilizes human relations and facilitates formation of social groups. Among all analyses of the concept of harmony, Yan Ying's soup allegory and its illustrative dialectical exposition is most impressive. *Zuozhuan* (Zuo Qiuming's Commentary on *"The Spring and Autumn Annals"*) says:

"Seeking harmony is like making soup. Water, fire, vinegar, soy sauce and prunes all go together to stew fish or meat. The chef makes a harmonious melange of these ingredients produce deliciously savory soup. In the process, he adds a little of this and a soupcon of that to bring its flavor and texture to perfection. The diner enjoys a good soup because it brings him enjoyment, hence peace. The interrelationship between ruler and courtier should correspond to this process. On observing that what the ruler believes to be right is flawed, the courtier points out wrong aspects, while endorsing those that are correct. On observing that what

the ruler believes to be wrong nevertheless has a valid aspect, the courtier points out that which is correct and rules out the wrong. In so doing governance retains its peace and harmony without vio-

lating the overall structure that keeps the masses free from competitiveness and contentiousness... Ancient sage-rulers adjusted the five flavors (sweet, sour, bitter, spicy and salty) when making soup and harmonized the five sounds (gong, shang, jue, zhi, yu — equivalent to the five-note scale in music, and in a metaphorical sense adhered to this process so as to ensure calmness of mind when handling state affairs.... But a problem arises when the ruler only pays heed to courtier Ju's view of what is right or wrong. This is like making soup without seasonings, when it is so tasteless no one wants it. It is also like re-peatedly playing the same note on the qin-se. This has no interest or enjoyment, so no one would want to listen to it..." (Cf. Zhaogong 20ᵗʰ Year)

As this allegory concludes, delicious soup cannot be made with a single ingredient, and fine music cannot be played on a single note. Soup made from a variety of ingredients has taste because it is an organic mixture of the five flavors, each distinct, but which blend to give an altogether richer and more appetizing piquancy. The same is true of music and the integrated melody of the five sounds. It is hence advantageous to bring in more ingredients as they produce better results when functioning under the principle of harmony.

Harmony is an essential concept:

First, it embodies a complementary relationship within which all the components are interactive and mutually beneficial. This is not only applicable to making soup and music; it also works when handling state affairs, as in the cooperation between ruler and courtier. In governance it serves to eliminate the wrong and emphasize that which

is right. In China, therefore, harmony is regarded as a crucial facet of leadership or political philosophy.

Second, harmony as a strategy connotes a dynamic process of creative transformation during which all the elements involved undergo a transformational synthesis, changing and collaborating but maintaining individual identity. Something entirely new is thus created.

Last but not least, harmony suggests a dialectic state in which opposites are united. This makes possible further growth and all the other positive aspects already mentioned. Yet, it must be pointed out that Yan Ying's description of harmony as a principle focuses only on the positive aspects of unity in opposites. His knowledge of dialectic relations revealed by means of harmony is limited, and therefore simplistic as he fails to detect the intrinsic conflict between opposites. In other words, his soup is one of harmonious proportions.

17

Similarly, his understanding of unity does not advance beyond the level of reconciliation. His philosophy is obviously aimed at providing a theoretical foundation for his political reformism.

To my mind, Yan Ying's reformism has validity when compared to those that are radical, destructive and imbued with bloodshed and anarchy.

CHAPTER THREE

The Delightful
Pursuit of Human Love

Language learners often comment about the difficulties they encounter with Chinese, in the sense of the ambiguity of some of its characters. This aspect is also true in the philosophical sense. The character *ren* (人), for instance, has the same pronunciation as another *ren* (仁). The former means person or human being, while the latter means humanity or human love. Since the structure of the second *ren* is composed of two people (二人), the human love it implies is often defined as reciprocal or bilateral benevolence. It is generated in social interactions between at least two people. *Ren* (仁) is believed to be born of mutual concern and understanding, and to foster good human relations.

In today's keenly competitive society, more and more people are aware of the significance of good human relations. Such relations are facilitated and sustained by what is referred to as human love (仁). It may be seen as an extension of individual self-love, first of all to family members, expressed as respect for the old and affection for

the young. It may further extend to neighbors, the community, and fellow workers, when all concerned strive to enhance their sense of belonging, mutual understanding, and close cooperation. There thus arises the *Dao* of *ren* (仁) as human love. The *Dao* itself is considered a cardinal virtue in Confucianism, embodying the overall spirit of Chinese philosophy.

So how does one pursue the *Dao* of *ren?* There are two guiding principles:

"Do not impose on others what you yourself do not desire" ; and

"Help others establish themselves insofar as you wish to establish yourself; and help others achieve their goals insofar as you wish to achieve yours."

The first principle exhorts you to put yourself in another's situation; that you treat others as you yourself would like to be treated. This nurtures unselfishness through not benefiting at the expense of the interests and feelings of others. The second principle advises broadening the mind and abiding by the rules of fair play. By so doing egoism is reduced and self-development towards self-perfection advances. This kind of *ren* is equivalent to fraternity, but can be further developed to the supreme level of "loving people and treasuring things" (*ren min ai wu*). At this point, the *Dao* of *ren* becomes universal love, toward human beings, and to all things under heaven. Within the current context of globalization this principle is of inestimable

value to social ecology, environmental ethics and sustainable development.

Historically the search for human love was one of the primary objectives of Neo-Confucianism during the Song Dynasty (960-1279), which encouraged a self-conscious reflection on "the delights of Confucius and Yan Hui" (*Kong-Yan le chu*). This delight came from rigorous pursuing the *Dao* of *ren* and is in two common quotations from *The Confucian Analects* (*Lunyu*). One is from Confucius himself : "*With coarse rice to eat, with only water to drink, and with my elbow for a pillow, I find delight in all. Wealth and honor attained*

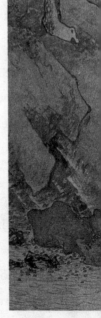

through immoral means have as much to do with me as
passing clouds." The other statement refers to his
favorite disciple Yan Hui: "*How admirable Hui is!*
A bowlful of rice to eat, a gourdful of water to drink, and
living in a mean dwelling; all this is hardship others would
find intolerable, but Hui does not allow it to affect his joy.
How admirable Hui is!"

How could Confucius and Yan Hui find delight and joy from such harsh living conditions?

23

What could be at the root of their rationale? There are three key possibilities. First, neither Confucius nor Yan Hui were ever depressed or in despair. Both were optimists (*le tian pai*), holding fast to a philosophical attitude toward the status quo that downplayed their plight. They appeared to maintain hope for the best when confronting the most difficult situations. Second, they were capable of self-reliance and tolerance, not in the sense of being content with what they were and what they had, but of being acceptant of whatever destiny might bring them. They thus delighted in and were attuned to their fate as predetermined by Heaven (*le tian zhi ming*). Lastly, they took such delight

in their pursuit of the *Dao* of *ren* that they forgot about their poverty-stricken state and thus freed themselves from care and worry. They enjoyed the *Dao* for the ability it gave them to make light of meager provisions in daily life (*an pin le dao*). What they sought from the *Dao* was enlightenment, and they were ready to sacrifice their lives to this end. As

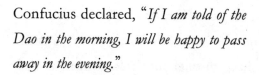

Confucius declared, "*If I am told of the Dao in the morning, I will be happy to pass away in the evening.*"

Incidentally, it is wrong to conclude that Confucius made no distinction between poverty and wealth, or that he was uncaring about being rich or poor. He stressed that poverty and low status are what men dislike, whereas wealth and high status are what men desire. If one cannot become rich and honored in the righteous way, one should remain carefree and enjoy one's life as it is. Confucius was always prepared to improve his living conditions in a material sense. Once he went so far as to admit that he would be willing to work as a guard wielding a whip outside the marketplace if it were possible for him to gain wealth by so doing. But as it happened, he followed his natural inclination towards study and pursuing the *Dao*.

In short, "*the delight of Confucius and Yan Hui*" is mainly attributed to conscientious devotion to the *Dao* of *ren*, and also to a firm sense of personal dignity in the face of hardship. This is peculiar to the "gentle man" or "man of virture" (*jun zi*), a character idealized throughout Confucianism and expressed by Mencius as the "great man" (*da zhang fu*). Such a person is supposed to possess three basic virtues: (1) Neither riches nor honors can corrupt him; (2) Neither poverty nor lowly conditions can make him swerve from his principles; (3) Neither threats nor force can bind him. All this is easier said than done. It can be accomplished only by cultivating a humane sense of values and strong moral volition.

CHAPTER FOUR

The Great
and the Small

All living things are different — in species, individual characteristics and other factors. Stretch out a hand before you, and you see five fingers of different lengths. If you attempt to modify your hand by making the long fingers shorter or pulling at the shorter ones to lengthen them, you are bound to suffer unbearable pain and frustration because this conflicts with nature.

Take other living beings. For example, a duck's legs are short, but if you try to lengthen them, the duck will feel pain. The crane's legs, on the other hand, are long, but if you try to shorten them the crane will suffer. Even if this alteration could be achieved with the help of modern biotechnology, neither the duck nor the crane would feel comfortable with their distorted physiognomies.

These observations indicate that different beings have their own innate talents, and are happy and at ease when exercising the full and free extent of their natural aptitudes. Inherent abilities and the achievements they produce are generally regarded as corresponding in magnitude to the largeness or smallness of their host. This is analogously illustrated by the following extract from *The Happy Excursion* (*Xiao yao you*) by Zhuang Zi (Chuang-tzu):

In the Northern Ocean is a fish called the *kun*,

which is thousand of miles in length. This fish metamorphoses into a bird called the *peng,* whose wingspan is many thousand miles in breadth. When the bird is in flight, its wings obscure the sky like clouds, and after descending to the Southern Ocean, it skims along the water for 3000 miles before ascending to a height of 90,000 miles. The wind beneath it and the blue sky above, it then mounts the wind and starts heading south. A cicada and a young dove laughed about the *peng,* saying: *"When we make the effort, we can fly up to a tree, but sometimes we fall to the ground midway. What is the point of going up 90,000 miles and then flying south?"* A quail also laughed, saying: *"Where does that bird think its going? I spring up with a bound to no more than a few yards high and then come down again. I just fly about among the brushwood or bushes, but to me this is perfect flying."*

What this story suggests is seemingly clear but

29

actually ambiguous. On the one hand, we see the enormous difference between the great and the small in their respective features, abilities and pursuits. In both size and natural ability the *peng* symbolizes the great while the quail and its like represent the small. The *peng* has large wings, which take it high and far, while the quail has tiny wings, and therefore flies low, and only for short hops.

Accordingly, their experience and achievements differ. The *peng's* deportment appears grand

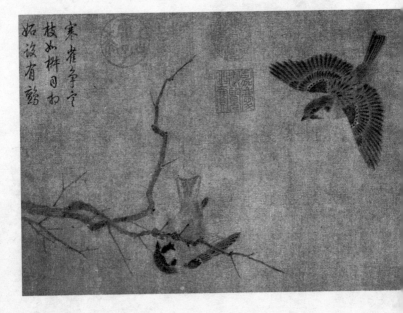

and daring, in contrast to that of the quail, which seems decidedly unimpressive. But each does what it needs to for its own purposes. If either goes against nature and tries to imitate the other's way of life, distress and frustration will certainly follow. Satisfaction with one's life achievements is therefore relative.

On the other hand, as the great *peng* and the small quail are different by nature, they live and behave according to the dictates of their instincts

and innate capacities. They both enjoy what they do to the full extent. Regardless of whether they are capable of short — or long-distance flight, their respective modes suit them. Content with what they are equipped to do, this satisfaction accords with their natural abilities. They may be compared with two guests at a royal banquet, both of whom enjoy themselves to the full extent, even though one's appetite is large and the other's small. The moral of

31

both these stories indicates the principle "equality in all things" (*qi wu*) as advocated by Daoist philosopher Zhuang Zi.

When there is equality in all things, no distinction is made between the great and the small, and no value judgment is ever made about anything. This disregard for so-called value corresponds with the Daoist notion of spiritual freedom. It is intended not merely to free people from the shackles of fame and fetters of profit, but to make them embrace the philosophy of non-action (*wu wei*). When fully comprehended, non-action is beneficial because it encourages people to proceed according to their natural abilities, and to do

what comes naturally to them. They are therefore wise enough not to take any misguided action or become involved in any inappropriate competition in order to be counted among whom they regard as the great. This does not necessarily entail giving up motivation towards self-realization or self-development in all possible aspects. The value system antithetical to Daoism, but most commonly followed, can be negative or even damaging, as within it are those whose complacency prevents them from realizing their full potential, and others self-effacing to the extent that they regard themselves progressing beyond the mundane. From a social perspective, neither attitude is desirable.

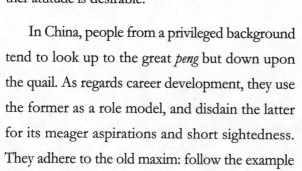

In China, people from a privileged background tend to look up to the great *peng* but down upon the quail. As regards career development, they use the former as a role model, and disdain the latter for its meager aspirations and short sightedness. They adhere to the old maxim: follow the example of the great, and disregard the modest aspirations of the small. This is valid, as long as it accords with the natural order of ability and suitability.

CHAPTER FIVE

Paradise in
Sudden Enlightenment

The pinnacled churches throughout the European continent, and the communicants within making silent devotions to lit candles are generally a source of awe and reverence to visitors from the Far East. This is a scenario in direct contrast to the crowded, bustling temples of China, where

worshipers burn incense and maké fervent wishes, some kneeling and kowtowing, to brightly painted statues of Buddha or Bodhisattva.

Chinese people are not religious, in the sense of worship for its own sake. This does not, however, inhibit large numbers of them, particularly in rural areas, from performing ritual obeisance based on the concept of luck, and superstition for entirely practical purposes. Stories of miracles abound at the temple. A woman declared barren bears a healthy baby (generally a son) as a result of her constant prayers to the Bodhisattva *Guanyin*, and is so convinced of the power of the Bodhisattva that she uses her own experience to convert others. The other extreme occurs when disappointment makes one whose prayers have apparently been ignored pour scorn on their erstwhile icon.

What significance, then, does Buddhism have to the Chinese in general? To sincere followers, it is "the paradise of supreme happiness" (*ji le shi jie*). According to descriptions in certain sutras, this paradise is one flowing with rivers that refresh

Guan Yin

the spirit with the many sweet fragrances exuding from bunches of flowers, dewed with jewels, floating along it. All beings there are free from misery and so enjoy pure happiness. Here there is no sin,

37

misfortune, distress, sadness or mortality.

From a Buddhist point of view, human life has two possible states. Mortal life is perceived as the fountainhead of suffering. It is termed the bitter sea (*ku hai*) from which no one can escape. But it does offer the possibility of a Utopia, characterized by a beautiful environment, and happiness born of release from care, worry and social ills. In so doing it is hoped to instill in followers a sense of hope that will endorse their convictions, rather than plunge them into a morass of total despair. There is also instruction on how to reach this paradise on completion of a certain procedure, and a long period of spiritual cultivation. The portrayed paradise is inviting, but to the pragmatic, value-orientated Chinese its "entry procedure" is simply not feasible.

Zen (Chinese Chan) Buddhism provides a simpler alternative for finding

spiritual paradise that is assumingly accessible to all

its followers: it is sudden enlightenment (*dun wu*).

This is a special kind of wisdom or *prajna* based

on negation of the temporal world and the belief

that all have the potential bodhi or innate ability to attain Buddhahood or Buddhata. Within this philosophy, the paradise of supreme happiness is secured immediately upon enlightenment. It is possible to approach Buddhahood by preserving and nourishing the potential bodhi while simultaneously pursuing everyday activities. Confinement to religious rituals is not required, as these are seen as nothing more than formal pretensions. Chan Buddhism thus directs the attention to an inner, rather than external, paradise.

Sudden enlightenment requires non-attachment to external objects, this being regarded as the foundation of all spiritual freedom. It also requires the ability to suspend thought, so as to maintain an open mind. According to the sixth Patriarch *Hui Neng*, the principle of sudden enlightenment means understanding and achieving wisdom without going through any complex, gradual procedure. From this point of view, understanding is natural and comes spontaneously. Enlightenment occurs when a mind has been purified and is void of all desire. The mind is enlightened through the abandonment of all elements of existence (*dharmas*) and by keeping itself empty, and therefore open. Sudden enlightenment means detachment from emptiness on becoming aware of emptiness, and also detachment from the absence of emptiness. In the same way, it means detachment from the self on becoming aware of it and also detachment from the absence of the self. On reaching this level, the state of *Nirvana* is possible.

What, then, happens on attaining sudden enlightenment? According to Chan Masters, at this stage, the person concerned is supposed to "step over the top of the hundred-foot bamboo" (*bai chi gan tou, geng jin yi bu*). In so doing, they will fall down to the opposite side of the bamboo they originally climbed in search of enlightenment. There is then nothing more expected of this person. They live their life in the normal way, pursuing accustomed activities. After enlightenment, however, old things are seen from a new perspective, as although the enlightened person may do nothing different from

41

what they did previously, they themselves are no longer the same. Say, they are freed from all conventional bonds and therefore live a life of spiritual freedom.

Chinese culture lacks divinity in a rigid religious sense. Its philosophies and religions have blurred boundaries. Chinese scholars think about philosophy in the spiritual sense and about religion philosophically. As regards the state of happiness, philosophy and religion often overlap in a mutual focus on the human condition.

Notes:

[1] Cf., *Aparimitayus Sutra* (*Amituo jing*), and *Sukhavativyuha Sutra* (*Dawuliangshou jing*), etc.

[2] Cf., "The *Zen* (*Chan*) School," in Wing-tsit Chan (tr.). *A Source Book in Chinese Philosophy*. (Princeton/New Jersey: Princeton University Press, 1963), p.441.

CHAPTER SIX

Loving People and Treasuring Things

The sandstorms that sweep through China's inland generally strike hardest in the North. Beijing suffers the most. Spring in the capital — that short, precious respite between a bitterly cold winter and five months of torrid summer — is frequently shrouded in a dull yellow pall of invading sandstorms.

Their frequency has increased dramatically over the last three years. In the spring of 2001 Beijing was hit by nine storms. It was pointless to go out on spring excursions at the weekends, as the landscapes was sullied by a sand infested yellow sky that rendered flowers and trees beaten and colorless. It was no pleasure for Beijing ladies to step out in their best and prettiest dresses, so their spring wear consisted of a veil over the face to keep flying dust out of eyes and noses. Everyone stayed indoors, but despite all windows and doors being securely shut there was nonetheless an odor of dust in homes and workplaces. Rampant sandstorms thus deprived everyone of seasonal springtime pleasure.

On April 12, 2003, *China Daily* reported the first large-scale sandstorm of the year to hit Northwest China. It swept through a 1.9 million sq. km area, its sand-drifts adversely affecting the everyday lives of 29.8 million people, and dangerously impeding agricultural production in the region. Beijing was, however, spared thanks to the acce-

leration of afforestation projects over recent years
and unseasonably high spring rainfall. It is to be
hoped that this reprieve from normal spring suffering might promote greater awareness of eco-
environmental protection and the interrelationship
between man and nature.

Considering environmental issues in terms of
the interaction between man and nature is remi-
niscent of a general aspect of Chinese philosophy.
Probably one of its most fundamental principles is

what Mencius called *ren min ai wu* (仁民爱物), loving people and treasuring things. The prerequisites for living according to this principle are an understanding of *tianli* (天理) — natural laws, and cultivating *renxin* (仁心) — a humane mind. *Tianli* could mean the heavenly *Dao* or universal principles, and *renxin,* benevolence and altruism. Knowledge of *tianli* promotes rational use of natural resources, and cultivation of *renxin* conduces to the habit of treating all people and things with equal consideration. The former demands investigation into the interactions between all things, leading to vision and insight. The latter requires kind-heartedness and sincerity. Both also call for a sense of vocation, and an awareness of the essential reciprocity between people and things. Human beings are part of nature, and as susceptible

as all other living creatures to intrusions that impact on the whole ecology. Yet humans have a
negative impact on nature, for example, by giving
less than appropriate priority to afforestation, and
exerting insufficient control over goat husbandry
in the interests of profit. If this should be allowed
to go on indefinitely, the Mongolian grassland will
become completely desertified, and sandstorms
will continue to strike the Northern regions, causing devastating damage to agriculture and the com-
munities that live there.

The human mentality and its ability to think
and reason, therefore, plays a vital role in dissemi-
nating *tianli*, or in this case, environmental awareness, and *renxin* as kindheartedness, and sincerity,
the combination of which promotes the belief in
loving people and treasuring things, either on a
socio-cultural or eco-environmental basis. When
human mentality concentrates solely on human
welfare, it overlooks the danger of overexploitation
of natural resources. The consequences of this
blinkered outlook are evident in our eco-develop-

ment having been thrown out of balance, and the current threat to the eco-environment. One example in China is the environmental disaster of desertified grassland — the result of excessive grazing — which is at the root of the recent increase in sandstorms. This vicious cycle calls for vigorous cultivation of *renxin* — the humanity and, *tianli* — environmental awareness.

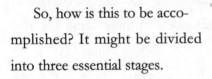

So, how is this to be accomplished? It might be divided into three essential stages.

The first is to take Zhang Zai's advice:"*da qi xin, yi ti tian xia zhi wu*"(大其心，以体天下之物). This is a basic attitude."*Da*"(大) means "great," opposite of its binary counterpart "*xiao*"(小) meaning "small"; "*xin*"(心)refers to "*renxin*"(人心), kindheartedness. Hence "*da qi xin*"(大其心) suggests that human beings must do their utmost to "make the mind great." Hypothetically, the mind is broad enough to accommodate the whole universe (人心之大，可以囊括宇宙). Yet the universe is believed not to limit or separate itself from humankind as long as humankind models itself upon it. This mind/universe relationship is of course metaphorical/spiritual rather than spatial/physical. Its transcendental pursuit can render the human mental capacity much greater and larger than anything else, and thus enable the human race to "experience and understand the real condition of all things under the sky, in the whole universe"(以体天下之物). "The real condition" embodies the state of the living environment that affects directly or indirectly the human condition. "To experience and understand the real condition" is not possible without relevant knowledge and an element of empathy. Knowledge comes from investigating and understanding the connections between all the things and, once

this has been achieved, empathy is the byproduct. Only when this state of mentality has been achieved is it possible to include oneself in the concept of "all things in the whole universe" and naturally develop a consciousness of the need to treasure them. Zhang Zai's statement also has negative implications. He calls on humanity to make its mind great simply because it is generally very small, confined to the narrow human domain of personal gains and losses, with nothing to spare for the animal, plant and marine kingdoms, let alone maintenance of their environment. Such smallmindedness amounts to egocentricity and anthropocentrism — hence the call to cultivate the human mind, or humane mentality.

Consequently, efforts must be redoubled to apply the second strategy. That is, "*xu qi xin, yi shou tian xia zhi shan*"(虚其心，以受天下之善). The literal translation of "*xu qi xin*"(虚其心) is "making the mind empty." It means emptying the mind of egocentricities, and cultivating modesty and openness. On achieving this state, it is possible to *"receive and appreciate all the good in the world"* (以受 天下之善). Goodness of this kind emanates not simply from human social activity; it is also part of the capacity of other life forms. In order to do the best for the whole it is necessary to learn from the virtues and merits of others. This entails appreciation of the benefits that other life forms within nature bring, and consideration of what may be done to enrich them. The principle of reciprocity, as condensed into the adage, one good turn deserves another thus applies. For instance, no human being can survive without the oxygen produced by plants. This is incentive to take care of plant life, because in so doing the human race may continue to breathe, and if it fails to acknowledge this, it will not survive.

The third strategy is to *"jin qi xin, yi mou tian xia zhi shi"* (尽其心，以谋天下之事). By *"jin qi xin"* (尽其心) is meant: to "complete the mind" by reverting to its original state(本心) or the good mind (良心), while the other is to "do the utmost through the mind"(尽心) by taking the right action.

Within Confucianism it is believed that the mind is inherently good, but that it might be misled by human desire. Its original good state might be regained if desire is reduced and eventually eliminated. This demands a cultivation process imbued with moral sincerity that culminates in the ability to *"plan and conduct all world affairs"* (以谋天下之事). In fulfilling this mission, it is possible to apply the correct mentality and follow the logical order by making the mind great enough to experience and understand all things in the universe. This is achieved, as stipulated by Zhang Zai, by making the mind empty so that it can receive and appreciate all the good in the world and, above all, love people and treasure things in unison. Loving people probably comes more naturally to humans than treasuring things, but the spiritual scope of humanity is seriously constricted when it ignores or overlooks the need to treasure things nonhuman. In this regard, Mencius proposed that *"If close knit nets are not allowed to enter deep pools and ponds, the fishes and turtles will multiply until ample is left for food; if*

axes and saws enter the hills and forests only at the appropriate time, there will be more than adequate timber for all uses."(数罟不入洿池，鱼鳖不可胜食也；斧斤以时入山林，材木不可胜用也). What Mencius was advocating was the principle of appropriateness and self-control. If humankind employs the wisdom for which it has the capacity, and rids the world of such scourges as sandstorms, the world will then be a better place to live for all concerned.

Notes:

According to official statistics, the extent of excessive animal husbandry in China constitutes 36.1 % of the total area, including Inner Mongolia Autonomous Region, Ningxia Hui Autonomous Region, Gansu, Qinghai, Tibet Autonomous Region and Xinjiang Uygur Autonomous Region.

CHAPTER SEVEN

Be Spring
to All Things

One old saying that is particularly rooted in the Chinese consciousness is "Spring is the most meaningful season." It has particular significance in rural regions, where spring is the time for plowing, and for planning the work for the coming year. In urban areas, peach and plum blossom and the fresh green shoots that clothe winter-denuded trees signify the time for outings and enjoyment of the warmer weather. One aspect of this season that adds greatly to the overall aesthetic is the sight of young girls, having finally put aside their warm winter wear, dressed in light colorful fabrics that display their maidenly charms to full effect. All in all, from the Chinese point of view, spring is a time of color, charm and cheer.

A developed appreciation of the resplendent beauties of spring can lead to an ability to be "spring to all things" (*yu wu wei chun*). This concept reflects the naturalistic humanism of Daoist Zhuangzi. The word "with" (*yu*) indicates the interaction between X and Y, a subject and an object, or put another way, a human contemplator of that under contemplation. "Things" (*wu*) means nature in all its glory — mountains and waters, flowers and trees, animals and birds, stars and clouds, and moonlight and sunshine. These aspects of nature are manifestations of pure, intrinsic beauty. Their negative counterparts are seen in the artificial distinction, in the holistic sense, between life and death, fortune and misfortune, wealth and poverty, worth and worthlessness, and praise and blame. These comparisons are based on relative value judgments. They link up all too neatly with everyday preoccupations with gain and loss that distress and pervade the consciousness, banishing any prospect of spiritual tranquility.

Then, what is meant by "be spring" (*wei chun*) in this context? "Spring" (*chun*) is the season of vitality, warmth and joy. It is often a symbol of hope, of fresh prospects and aspirations. Here, however, it refers specifically to a harmonious interrelationship between man and nature, an interactive current of optimism and good will between the perceivable environment and the inner self. In this sense, if you love nature, it will never betray you. Yours is a symbiotic relationship. A tree planted in springtime brings a blessedly cool shade in high summer. Hence, to "be spring to all things" is to be in harmony with one's surroundings and so enjoy their beneficence. It denotes a naturalistic awareness of the role all things in nature play, and a humanistic attitude toward the super-moral development of the human "perfect character" (*caiquan*).

This "perfect character" is attained when the consciousness successfully sustains a state of peace, born of the contentment that a true appreciation of nature brings. It entails freeing the mind from valueoriented egoism. In following the laws of nature it is possible to observe the paths of destiny, and avoid suffering the social ills and human troubles stemming from a blinkered assessment of right and wrong from the standpoint of personal favor and interests. The ultimate ideal is Zhuangzi's concept: Insignificant and small is that by which you belong to humanity (*miao hu xiao zai, suo yi shu yu ren ye*). Grand and great is that by which you identify with nature (*ao hu da zai, du cheng qi tian*). In

the former sense, a person is trapped within the confines of the "small I" by taking man as the measure of all things and bound exclusively to human affairs, unaware of the greater role of allembracing nature. In the latter, sublimation has occurred from moving out of the "small I" to the "Big We" and a conscious identification with nature. In other words, your horizon broadens to a holistic outlook on the interdependence between humankind and nature, rather than making judgments based on material egoistic values. This stage brings the kind of spiritual freedom to take, in Zhuangzi's terminology, *the happy excursion* (*xiao yao you*), whereby you may "Wander, free and at ease with all things around" (*cheng wu yi you xin*), and "mount the clouds of heaven, ride on the sun and the moon, and thus roam at ease beyond the four oceans" (*chen yun qi, qi ri yue, er you hu si hai zhi wai*). All this signifies a momentum that transcends the finite human world, allowing entry into the cosmic world of infinitude. The ultimate enlightenment is where "Heaven and Earth and I come into existence together, and all things are one with me" (*tian di yu wo bing sheng, er wan wu yu wo wei yi*). This phantasm of absolute freedom without boundaries is characterized by the oneness of man and the universe, which is attainment of the omnipotent *Dao*, or in a similar sense, the ideal life.

Even though Zhuangzi's advice to "be spring to all things" is inspiring as regards promoting awareness of the mutual beneficence of the inter-relationship between humans and nature, I personally find it exaggeratedly idealistic, and therefore practically unachievable. But it may still be adopted as a general attitude, wherein nature is regarded in a fourfold manner: in the ontological sense, where humans are a part of nature, which in turn nourishes humankind as a whole; in the epistemological sense, where nature constitutes a body of knowledge requiring boundless investigation, and which is a constant source of new discoveries; ecologically, where nature is to be properly protected and utilized in order to achieve sustainable development; and aesthetically, where nature is the primal source of all beauty. The aesthetic aspect relates to the Kantian concept of "disinterested contemplation," wherein discovery of the myriad forms of nature's beauty makes possible the projection of feelings and emotions into such aesthetic contemplation. The mundane is thus sloughed off, and human empathy is exchanged for natural sympathy, which brings psychical catharses. In today's world , where we are so vulnerable to such real threats as terrorist attack and SARS-like scourges, it is all the more necessary for us to maintain the spirit of spring with all that is beautiful in nature.

Notes:

The title "Be Spring to All Things" may first seem poorly worded. It did to me! But on reading the article, Zhuangzi's concept becomes clear. Be spring to all things is really the only way to express what he meant.

CHAPTER EIGHT

Practical Wisdom
in Horse Racing

June is a significant month in China as it is when the state university entrance exams take place. In Beijing over 80,000 participated in this highly competitive event on the June 7/8 weekend. Prior to the exams the media carried a wealth of brainstorming suggestions as to how examinees might perform to the best of their ability, one of which struck a particular chord in me. It encouraged participants to focus their time and energy on consolidating their strong subjects, rather than waste time on laborious revision of those at which they had low aptitude in the hope of scoring a few extra points.

Next year's examinees might consider this advice in the light of the ancient tale of the strategy employed by General *Tian Ji* in his annual horse race with the Lord of *Qi*.

The story goes that the Lord of *Qi* and General *Tian Ji* held a horse race every year. They selected three horses each that ran in pairs for three races. The owner of two out of three of the winners got a trophy. The Lord of *Qi* would consistently win as each of his horses ran a little faster each than the General's. One year, shortly before the race, General *Tian Ji* was at a loss as to how he might win the trophy from his Lord. Well-known strategist *Sun Bin* called to see him at this time, and on the General telling him about the race, his advice was to alter the racing sequence of his horses. The General accordingly pitted his third horse against the Lord's first — a race he was bound to lose. He then raced his first horse against the Lord's second, and won, and paired his second horse with Lord's third, winning again. He thus won two of the three races and collected the trophy for the first time.

What is the story's message? It indicates the importance of choosing the correct strategy for any kind of trial or test. In this case, it should first

be clarified that the Lord's three horses always ran respectively faster than the General's when in a preset order of first against first through to third against third. The Lord's first horse was the best and unbeatable, but his second was probably no better than the General's first, and his third certainly no better than the General's second. This being the case, the General was certain to lose at least one race no matter which of his three horses he matched against the Lord's first. So this time he changed his racing order, pairing his slowest horse with the Lord's fastest. He thus purposely lost one race, but won the other two and the overall victory. The strategy was that of being prepared to lose in order to win, whereby a small sacrifice is paid in order to achieve the greater glory. This is the superficial message, but on looking deeper another more subtle truth emerges. It is that of making the most of strengths and weaknesses according to the demands of any specific situation. This requires intelligence, but also the courage to create advantages out of disadvantages. The strategy also constitutes a

warning against mechanical conformity to routinized logic, advocating instead stepping off the beaten track.

At this point I am reminded of Lao Zi's philosophy on a similar theme. In his *Dao De Jing* (*Tao Te*

Ching) about the way and its power, he prescribes a series of metaphoric strategies. In Chapter 36, for instance, he arrives at the conclusion: "*In order to take, it is necessary first to give.*" The contemporary interpretation of this is that initial giving is expedient to the ultimate end of taking. It may often be observed that an ostensible giver is actually one who has enough patience to wait and take the lion's share when the time is ripe, like a fisherman using a tiny worm to hook a big fish. In this way, he is prepared to give a little at first in order to take more later on, as with General *Tian Ji*, who was prepared to lose the first race in order to win the following two.

In the same chapter, Lao Zi says: "*In order to contract, it is necessary first to expand. In order to weaken, it is necessary first to strengthen. In order to destroy, it is necessary first to promote ...This is called Subtle Light* (*wei ming*)." These ideas could be based on empirical observations and life experience. A flower, for instance, will naturally wither, or contract, after fully blossoming. Conversely, an inchworm draws itself together, contracting its body in order to gather strength, when about to stretch out and expand, thereby advancing its body. Lizards and snakes hibernate — a contraction of movement in winter — in order to preserve life until expanding into vitality in spring. It is therefore assumed in *The Great Treatise on The Book of Changes* that *"contraction and expansion act upon each other; hereby arises that which furthers."* This dialectical speculation indicates that everything has two aspects that are in a state of continuous opposition and mutual transformation. On one developing to its acme, it will inevitably transmute to its opposite. This assertion also suggests a strategy that may be applicable to personal development in today's complicated social environment. Very often we are confronted with the dilemma of whether to contract — to retreat or take no action — or to expand — to advance and act. This necessitates weighing up which will bring the greater benefit. As for the interrelationship between weakening and strengthening, it follows a similar logic to that of destroying and promoting. In today's ruthlessly competitive business world, for example, tricks are played and traps are set. Someone might be promoted specifically to handle a thorny task, but on accomplishing it and starting to plan a bright future, be kicked out or cast aside on the pretext that the task in question is no longer relevant. They might also be promoted for the sole purpose of expediting something no one else wants to take responsibility for, like getting rid of another operative, or signing a contract that offends a longstan-ding client or associate.

Such strategies prevail in the political arena, and Lao Zi himself has been described as a political conspirator. Certain scholars argue that this interpretation is based on a purposely conventional misreading or misconception. It is only feasible on the premise that each reader forms his own image of Lao Zi in the light of personal opinions and contemporary parallels to his philosophy, which are, and will continue to be relevant to any period of history. Lao Zi appears to focus on such dialec-tical interactions in order to illustrate his concept of the inexorable transformations of opposites.But he is actually more concerned about natural phenomena than human affairs, as he consistently seeks to demonstrate how the *Dao* of Heaven or the natural law works in binary or bipolar situations. Citing him as a conspirator in any negative sense is hence groundless. Furthermore, it is possible through Lao Zi's perspective to gain insight into the natural movement and transformational features of all things. As already observed, that given is a facet of that taken; expansion signals the imminence of contraction; and promotion can be at the root of destruction. Similarly, the strong grows

out of the weak; and abundance is harbinger of decline. Both natural phenomena and human affairs develop and change in this dialectically inevitable fashion.

71

What Lao Zi calls the Subtle Light (*wei ming*) may be the kind of practical wisdom displayed by General *Tian Ji*, meaning the pragmatism necessary for self-achievement and self-development. The rich store of such wisdom within Chinese philosophy should be explored and rediscovered in the contemporary socio-cultural context.

CHAPTER NINE

The Sage Wisdom
of Reversion

In the previous chapter we had a discussion on practical wisdom, with particular reference to a story about horse racing. This chapter we look at sage wisdom from a different perspective. If practical wisdom deals specifically with practical issues and interests, sage wisdom is relevant to

matters of a spiritual nature, but not in the religious sense. In this context, spiritual refers to a way of life whose innermost dimension is based on a dialectical thought process that creates a sensitivity to and wariness of excess, or radical action.

Even today there are contemporary Chinese sages who maintain superficial calm when tremendously excited or happy over, say, career advancement or a huge win on the lottery. This indicates their awareness of the hidden power of reversion as exemplified in the empirical aphorisms: *le ji sheng bei* (Extreme happiness turns to misery) and *wu ji bi fan* (Movement to one extreme is bound to cause a reversal to the other). This means they mentally train

themselves to treat good or bad matters in a philosophical manner, likening them to a pendulum swing. They are then psychologically prepared for the worst in the midst of happy events, and expect a change for the better when hit by disaster or tragedy. This is not to say that they act upon the principle of the golden mean (*zhong yong*), but that they follow the principle of reversion (*fan*). According to Lao Zi, pledged founder of early Daoism:

"*Reversion is the movement of the Dao*" (*fan zhe dao zhi dong*).

The Chinese concept of *fan* is a dynamic term meaning twofold. It refers in one sense to the interrelationship between opposites, and in another to a return to the root that is the unity of opposites, meaning transformation and change. That the movement of the *Dao* is thought of as reversion is demonstrated by the Tai Ji (literally translated

Great Acme), in which the two forces of *Yin* and *Yang* are constantly and simultaneously in motion, interdependent and interactive. History is witness to the phenomenon of how a nation, its culture, economic strength and political power are doomed to decline once it reaches its acme, when it then undergoes a reversion within an ever-changing process. A flower in full bloom is as certain to whither as are the young to grow old. When considering the environment, the visible changes in plants and the stages of their life cycle are sufficient to endorse the concept of dialectical move-

ment of the *Dao* as a natural law. The *Dao* observes: *"Things too lofty too easily fall down; things too white too easily stain; songs too highbrow have few listeners; reputations too high fall far short of reality."* In this context the degree of tooness is tantamount to extremeness or excessiveness and as such likely to trigger off a reversal in diametric opposition to the existing state of affairs. This conforms to the Chinese concept of inevitable reversion on reaching an extreme.

The chief benefit of *fan* as reversion lies not merely in its emphasis on opposing interrelationships and the role it enacts in their transformation. Its focus on the return of all things to the root that is their final destination is also significant. There at the root is where the unity of opposites occurs, and where all potential conflicts and antitheses are resolved. This is the idealized function and state of *fan* as reversion. Reversion itself must be facilitated and reinforced by effort as well as favorable conditions — a passive wait-and-see attitude is insufficient. It is also imperative to be able to recognize the objective existence of two aspects of the developmental process. Appropriate handling of any situation means avoiding bias. Awareness of inevitable reversion means taking into account both sides and keeping an eye on the dynamic change that occurs on the verge of interaction between opposites. In so doing the chance may be grasped and an advantageous position maintained. An objective stand is essential because subjective egoism or wishful thinking will inevitably push matters to an extreme.

A deep understanding of the principle of reversion is believed to be the key to sage wisdom. This is the highest form of wisdom when the sageness within (*nei xing*) is construed as an aspect of man's highest possible achievement. It provides enlightenment and guidance, perceptibly and imperceptibly, to human existence as it nurtures the spirit. When considering the pursuit of pleasure, for example, sagely wisdom observes: "*The five colors blind the eyes. The five tones deafen the ears. The five flavors jade the palate. Racing and hunting send one insane.* " The five colors and tones refer to the arts, such as painting and music, the five flavors are delicious food, racing and hunting are types of entertainment or leisure activity. All may be enjoyed, but excessive indulgence leads to a negative or even destructive influence on taste, the physical body and the soul. This is a moral warning to those who wallow in sensuous enjoyment or a hedonistic way of life. Many cases of corruption exposed in the media today reveal how those involved are addicted to free luxuries and pleasures. Their state of euphoria induced by easy access to privilege prevents them from perceiving the risks attaching to this intemperate lifestyle.

On the pursuit of fame and wealth, the sage wisdom of reversion says: *"An excessive love of fame is bound to engender extravagance. A rich hoard of wealth is bound to suffer a heavy loss."* [2] Any observer of society would agree that people most desire and pursue fame and wealth, and that the price they often pay is alienation or enslavement *"The reins of fame and the shackles of wealth"* (*ming jiang li suo*) mean forfeiting spiritual freedom, something the avaricious and the fame-seeking should bear in mind before going to extremes. The most realistic Chinese people acknowledge the social kudos of fame, and how wealth relieves economic stress, yet they are the very last to grasp at or grovel for either. To their mind, life's true value lies in its spiritual freedom.

On the potential development of a particular being, the sagely wisdom of reversion holds that *"The tender can overcome the hard, and the weak can overcome the strong."* [3] This is a recommendation to *"keep to the tender and weak"* and to develop further so as eventually to prevail over *"the firm and the strong.* " The analogy of drops of water wearing a hole in stone over time immediately springs to mind. Consistency in endeavor eventually brings about a dramatic change. If it is absent, the tender and the weak remain so, as do the firm and the strong. There is no meeting and melding of opposites.

On social discourse, the sagely wisdom of reversion affirms that *"True words are not beautiful; beautiful words are not true.* " [4] The implication here is that it is best to be a good listener in the sense of distinguishing the true from the false, the good from the evil, and the beautiful from the ugly. Otherwise, it is all too easy to fall into the trap of believing the beautiful words so extravagantly bandied about in today's self-promoting society.

In conclusion, the sagely wisdom of reversion works on different levels toward different orientations. It helps to fulfill non-practical needs and to fulfill spiritual purposes. Those pursuing self-transcendence are liable to flounder, but cultivation of sagely wisdom may enhance the artistic course of human life, which in turn brings spiritual freedom. Completion of this process is by no means easy or attainable. It can only be achieved through maintaining an appropriate attitude born of renouncing the ego and excessive desire. This is no mean feat in today's temptationridden society.

Notes:

[1] Cf. Lao Zi. *Dao De Jing (Tao-Te Ching)*. Ch. 12.

[2] Ibid., Ch. 44.

[3] Ibid., Ch. 78.

[4] Ibid., Ch. 81.

CHAPTER TEN

The Heavenly Way
and the Human Way

Having never worshipped the godhead, China's population is generally regarded as atheist. Religion is not, however, an alien concept. People frequently exclaim "Good Heavens!" (*tian na*) and "Good Lord!" (*lao tian ye a*). To their mind, *tian* — Heaven — is perceived on the one hand as the supreme force that rules the universe, and on the other as the spiritual entity to whom they bring their cares and worries. They call out to Heaven on encountering something unexpected, mysterious or unprecedented, often as a way of letting off steam. On occasion, however, oaths, or vows

Lao Zi

to pursue a purpose, are made in the name of Heaven, making it an unseen witness, adding impetus to accomplishing the task at hand.

From a philosophical point of view, Heaven as a spiritual entity has ethical significance within Taoism and its principle of *tian dao* —the Heavenly Way. There are various concepts of the Heavenly Way, two of which represent the fundamental Chinese view of spirituality and moral values.

The first concept is rooted in Taoism and its philosophy of acting in accordance with nature. From a Taoist perspective, the Heavenly Way is natural law. It is hence spontaneous, letting everything be what it is, or become what it can be naturally, without interference or influence. It is regarded as the heart of the universe because it benefits all things without causing harm. As defined by Lao Zi: *"The Heavenly Way resembles the drawing of a bow. When the string is too high, lower it. When it is too low, raise it. When too taut, slacken it. When too loose, tighten it. The Heavenly Way reduces excess and supplements insufficiency."* A bow is drawn in order to shoot an arrow, and aimed towards the target. The Heavenly Way is believed to be just in a way similar to the correct drawing and aiming of a bow. By holding fast to the principle of doing the right thing one never goes astray.

Confucius

Within the concept of the Heavenly Way exists unconditional equality, and therefore justice. Its principle of shunning extremes of strength and weakness, dominance and repression, wealth and poverty and abundance and dearth are relevant to social order. Eliminating social gaps, and preserving order and stability, it is perceived as a force that maintains harmony and equilibrium.

Within Taoism, The Human Way is in complete contrast to the Heavenly Way as it *"further reduces the insufficient,"* its emphasis being on *"excess."* In this context *"the insufficient"* and *"excess"* represent the two main social classes. The "insufficient" is the underprivileged stratum that lacks the means to maintain life. *"Excess"* is the privileged stratum with abundant living resources. In contrast to the justice, fairness and equality advocated by the Heavenly Way, within the Human Way *"the insufficient"* take on all manual labor and are condemned to toil in order to make ends meet. The *"excess"* have the power to exploit *"the insufficient,"* and consequently become richer and more powerful by en-

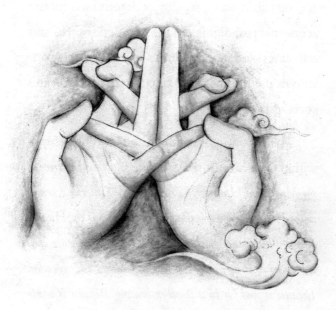

suring that *"the insufficient"* remain the underdogs.
The Taoist concept of the Human Way is therefore
comparable to the law of the jungle, prevalent
within modern civilization. A generally accepted
norm of conduct, the Human Way encourages the
greed and desire for material possessions, exploita-
tion, and class discrimination that ultimately culminates in social disorder. What, then, perpetuates
this negative Human Way? The power and social
structure of the institutional system; possession

and distribution of wealth as determined by the economic paradigm; and the competitiveness and selfishness inherent in human nature. All this constitutes the fountainhead of class stratification and social differentiation.

The second concept of the Heavenly Way is within Confucianism. As defined in *The Doctrine of the Mean and Harmony (Zhongyong)*, *"Sincerity (cheng) is the Heavenly Way; Reflecting on sincerity is the Human Way. Thus utmost sincerity is unresting. Because it is unresting so it perdures. Because it perdures so it goes far. Because it goes far so it is all-embracing. Because it is all-embracing so it is lofty and bright. Being all-embracing is the means by which it supports things; being lofty and bright is the means by which it protects things; going far is the means by which it accomplishes things. The way of heaven and earth may be completely summarized in one phrase: Its making things is without duplicity; its generating things is unfathomable. "* Sincerity is hence the basis of the Confucian Heavenly Way and Human Way. Sincerity denies duplicity. It forms a principle proceeding from the Heavenly Way that encompasses the virtues of being unresting and perduring , all-embracing and far-reaching, lofty and buight,and supportive and generative. Sincerity enacts all these virtues and nurtrres without claiming reciprocal merit or gain.

Reflecting on sincerity within the Confucian Human Way is beneficial in itself. It involves comprehension and contemplation of the nature of sincerity and an appreciation of its actual practice. From a human point of view, sincerity is at the basis of the five constant virtues of humanheartedness, righteousness, reciprocal etiquette, wisdom, and trustworthiness. It can be said to be the principle underlying morality. Sincerity is in turn preserved by human-heartedness, implemented by righteousness, promoted by reciprocal etiquette proprieties, nurtured by wisdom and justified by trustworthiness. The etymology of *cheng*, sincerity is *xin*(信), trustworthiness. The Chinese character *xin* consists of *ren* (a person) and *yan* (words), meaning the person matches the word and vice versa. It denotes moral interaction by representing a person of honor and words of truth. A person of honor keeps their promise and attaches importance to reality. Words of truth confirm reality and signify knowledge. This gives rise to integrity of deed and word (*yan xing he yi*), or synthesis of knowledge and practice (*zhi xing he yi*).

From both the Taoist and Confucian point of view, the Heavenly Way is above the Human Way. It provides a frame of reference and guide for the human pursuit of self-sublimation. According to Taoist expectations, the Human Way is negative but can be sublimated and transformed into the Sage Way (*sheng ren zhi dao*) if it acts according to the principles of the Heavenly Way. The Sage Way

"acts for others but never competes" (*wei er bu zheng*). Working on the supreme principle of equaling Heaven, or the Heavenly Way, the Sage Way nurtures others, helping them to develop without expectation of fame or profit. Its actual practitioner is the sage free from egoism, who is therefore pure and innocent.

This mental state is perceived within Taoism as the source of absolute spiritual freedom.

From a Confucian perspective, the Human Way is positive as it follows the principle of sincerity in order to merge with the Heavenly Way. Its ultimate purpose is that of becoming a sage. The sage is bestowed with a sense of mission and social commitment, prepared to do his utmost for the good of the whole regardless of personal interests. He will sacrifice everything to "prepare the mind for the universe, establish the Tao of morality for the people, carry forward the teachings of preceding sages, and pave the way for everlasting peace in the world (*wei tian di li xin, wei sheng min li ming, wei wang sheng ji jue xue, wei wan shi kai tai ping*)." The human mind that has successfully prepared itself for the universe is one with enhanced cognition, conversant with the law of the universe through sustained and consistent investigation of all things. It is therefore a universal mind that has transcended egoism, making it fit to enact moral codes of conduct for all people and things.

The Heavenly Way is symbolic. The Sage Way is idealistic. The Human Way gains value and significance upon embracing them both. Yet, achieving the ideal of sageness is no easy matter. Seeking it is like drawing a cake to sate hunger. Pursuit of this ideal nevertheless connotes acknowledgement of the need to stress and promote the virtues of selflessness and sincerity that are so conspicuously absent in today's profit-oriented and duplicity-ridden society.

CHAPTER ELEVEN

The Hierarchical
Realm of Being

Our approach to and expectations of life generally indicate our essential attitude and life motivations. An example is the following story about four of Confucius' disciples, and how they told him of their personal life aspirations:

On one occasion when Zi Lu, Zeng Xi, Ran You and Gongxi Hua were in the company of their master, Confucius, he encouraged them speak about their ideal mode of life, and what they would do if their abilities were truly appreciated. Zi Lu said, *"If I were to administer a state of a thousand chariots, situated between powerful neighbors, troubled by armed invasions and frequent famines, in three years I could give its people the courage and direction to overcome their difficulties."* Confucius smiled at him, and then asked Ran You to describe his desired pursuit. *"If I were to administer an area measuring sixty or seventy miles square,"* he said, *"I could, within three years, bring the size of the population up to an appropriate level. As to rites and music, I would leave that to abler gentlemen."* Confucius then turned to Gongxi Hua who said, *"I do not purport to have the necessary ability to fulfill my life's aims, but I am ready to learn. I should like to assist as a minor official in charge of protocol on ceremonial occasions at ancestral temples or diplomatic gatherings, properly dressed in ceremonial cap and robes."* Confucius nodded and then turned to Zeng Xi who was playing the lute, called the *se.*

After playing the last few notes he strummed the final chord, stood up and said, *"I differ from the other three in my life choices. In late spring, I would like to go on outings in newly made spring garments together with five or*

six friends and six or seven attendants. I would go bathing in the River Yi and enjoy the breeze on Rain Altar. On the way home I would sing and chant poetry. "Confucius sighed and said, *"I admire Zeng Xi's ambition."*

It may be observed that the first disciple Zi Lu's vocation is a political mission to secure good governance of a state, Ran You considers his social duty of promoting effective administration of an area, and Gongxi Hua's interest is in continuous learning and personal cultivation. In complete contrast to all three is Zeng Xi, whose desire is to live an artistic life, taking happy excursions into nature and luxuriating in the incomparable pleasure of chanting poetry and singing. This mode of life is one of freedom from any social confinement, and nurtures a personality independent of external material values. Confucius appreciates Zeng Xi's choice for its making an art form of life itself through music and poetry, eventually elevating it to an aesthetic kingdom of freedom. This was considered to be the highest state of being as it represents emancipation from all external bonds and brings a state of constant delight at the freedom to enjoy the arts of music and poetry.

According to *Li Zehou*, a research fellow at the Institute of Philosophy of the Chinese Academy of Social Sciences, the artistic or aesthetic realm of being encompasses all the joys of human freedom, fulfillment and humanity. Its key merit lies in transforming the rationalized social norms, or "rule by rites" into a truly human consciousness. That Confucius endorses Zeng Xi's choice demonstrates the extent of his aesthetic sensibility, and how he saw ancient music as a means of maintain ing social order through its development of an awareness of all facets of human nature.

In their preoccupation with the possibilities of human existence in general, contemporary Chinese thinkers endeavor to rediscover the relevant sources of Chinese philosophy on life. *Feng Youlan* (1895-1990), a professor of philosophy at Peking University, stood out for having defined the preceding four realms of being in terms of contemporary characteristic life styles and pursuits.

The first is the natural realm of being in which a person lives according to nature's way. It is an habitual mode of life followed by those with no clear concept of what they seek. They just do as they are accustomed and live according to convention, folklore, and customs, looking no further than their immediate needs. They might rise at sunrise to do unskilled manual work and rest at sunset, following natural cycles as did our primitive ancestors. They are the direct opposite of artists, who devote themselves to creative fantasies and become obsessed with art works. Artists may produce works of world significance that can only be created through manic inspiration born of an emotional surge. They are therefore spontaneous in all they do, stopping and starting instinctively rather than according to rationalized principles of causal conditions.

The second realm is that of utilitarianism, whose fundamental feature is the desire for material gain. Those embracing this state of being strive for personal achievement and profit. They single-mindedly pursue what they want, intent on finding ways through enterprise to acquire property, fame, and status. Highly rational, they know exactly how to achieve their objectives. The negative aspect of

the utilitarian is their self-centeredness, as they work entirely for their own gain. But on the positive side, they are persistent to the extent of being ready to sacrifice their lives for the actualization of their goals. They consequently bring about epoch-making events, take heroic action, and achieve groundbreaking progress. Many historical figures that have contributed to the welfare and benefit of others have been fundamentally utilitarian.

The third is the moral realm of being. Its practitioners lean toward collective rather than individual interests, considering the pursuit of the latter as selfish and unjust. They believe it righteous to work towards the common good. Highly aware that they are part of society, they preach and practice the principle of live and let live in the belief they can realize their own values only through serving society. They therefore act upon moral codes and social norms, integrating their own needs with those of others. They consequently seldom encounter social conflict, being perceived as givers and contributors in contrast to the utilitarian takers and possessors.

The fourth is the cosmic or universal realm of being that is based on a sense of mission to serve and help everything in the universe grow. Those of this realm regard themselves as personally committed to human society and the universe. Having a deep understanding of human nature, and the holistic relationship between humankind and the universe, they expend all their energy on *"loving people and treasuring things."* In a spiritual sense they think of themselves as the plural *"We"* rather than the singular *"I"* and thus live in a kingdom of freedom rather than one of necessity.

On reviewing these hypotheses, there arises a hierarchy: the natural state of being at the base, and the cosmic state topmost. These two extremities are uncommon in contemporary society, the natural state of being impractical and the cosmic state too idealistic. The utilitarian and moral realms, however, might be said to be the most realistic and applicable to life today. The majority of people would hence place themselves and their approach to life some where between the swings of utility and morality.

CHAPTER TWELVE

The Attitude towards Life and Death

"To be, or not to be, that is the question ..." to Hamlet and to the majority of people, who generally treasure life and fear death. In many cultures it is taboo to raise the topic of death in everyday discourse, but this is not the case with the Chinese people. To them life and death are a common

conversational topic. Their matter of fact approach illustrated in the sayings: *"Human life is nothing but a stage over which the sun and the moon function as two spotlights"* (人生一台戏，日月两盏灯); *"We live our lives in the same way as grass passes the seasons from spring to autumn"* (人生一世，草木一秋); *"There is no distinction between the old and the young among those on their way to the tomb"* (黄泉路上无老少); *"Life is not to be rejoiced as death is not to be resented"* (生而不乐，死而无怨).

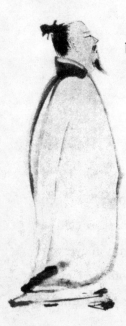

These aphorisms exemplify the belief that man is born to die, and that life is merely a journey from womb to tomb, a natural process governed by an objective law that no one can escape or flout. No matter what endeavors one might make, everyone succumbs to mortality within a certain time span. Nothing can be done other than to follow the natural process from birth to death, just as grass sprouts in spring like the essence of youth and withers in autumn like the onset of old age.

All this seems grimly realistic, even pessimistic, but is nevertheless an attitude accepted and widely shared among Chinese people. Awareness of the inevitability of death enables them to face it philosophically. Seeing human life as a facet of nature and the life cycle of grass as mirroring their own is actually optimistic, as it dispels the dread of death itself.

This naturalistic philosophy on life and death has its roots in Daoism. Its founder Lao Zi (Laotzu) perceived life and death as natural phenomena, the former not to be overvalued and the latter not to be dreaded. He says, uncompromisingly:

Man comes alive into the world

And goes dead into the earth.

Three out of ten will live long.

Three out of ten will live short.

And three out of ten will strive for long life

But meet premature death.

And for what reason?

It is because of excessive preservation of life.

Only those who don't value their lives are wiser

Than those who overvalue their lives.

I have heard that those who are good at preserving life

...are out of the range of death.[1]

This is the essential Daoist concept of the reality of life and death, where the materialistic rich and nobility are criticized for wasting their time on "excessive preservation of life" that usually ends in frustrati on Observant and critical, Lao Zi could do little other than adhere to his *Dao* of plainness and simplicity and advise others to preserve life by living their natural term free from cares and worries, outside and so going beyond *"the range of death."* The wise observation: *"Man comes alive into the world and goes dead into the earth* " leads to the conclusion that people should live life naturally so as to enjoy it to the full. They should neither be intimidated by a dread of death when it is in any event inevitable, nor overvalue life, as striving to preserve it is futile.

Zhuang Zi (Chuang-tzu), acknowledged successor to Lao Zi, continued to ruminate on the essence of human existence. His conclusion was that all living beings are born of *qi* — the vital energy or source of being. Human life is created from a *qi* cluster and ends when it disperses. Zhuang Zi went so far as to declare that life is but a tumor that death eradicates, seeing it as a process of becoming, toiling, suffering, retiring, and passing on to the grave that is the final resting place.

This could be construed as negative on the grounds that it encourages hopeless passivity at the prospect and inevitability of death, viewing life as something to be muddled through in the comforting knowledge, as described in the Chinese saying, that "*The misery one suffers in life is no worse or greater than the death of their heart* " （哀莫大于心

死). Waiting for the Damocles sword of death to fall and make an end of it means to be or not to be is no longer a question, as living life this way is in itself a kind of death.

From another point of view, however, the Daoist attitude toward death can engender a positive life stance. Acceptance of death's inevitability gives rise to a sense of meaning and purpose in life as the natural passage from birth to death, and motivation a person to make the most out of it, treasuring every minute. The knowledge that time is on the wing and can never be recaptured creates a sense of mission and social commitment. The resultant redoubling of effort and hard work so as to live life to the full extends the significance of an existence within society and into history. Transcending the mortal limitations that arise from the mystique of death thus makes it possible to handle hardship, difficulty, misery and suffering. This, in turn, creates a particular mindset, most obvious in revolutionaries and religious martyrs, who willingly devote their waking hours to worthy causes and sacrifice themselves for the sake of their ideals. In Confucianism there is also the idealized character *jun zi* (superior man), who is expected to give up his life unthinkingly in the interests of preservation and advancement of humanity. Such a spirit of devotion can arise only from a positive conception of death.

Put in a nutshell, the Daoist belief is that true spiritual freedom lies in understanding the nature of death and living without fear of it, according to the *Dao* of being, rather than being enslaved and petrified by the specter of death. It encourages people to be masters of their own fate, so improving their quality of existence and achieving spiritual freedom. In conclusion, here is another quotation from Lao Zi, for the sake of self-reflection:

> *When the highest type of literati hear of the Dao,*
>
> *They diligently practice it.*
>
> *When the average type of literati hear of the Dao,*
>
> *They half believe it.*

When the lowest type of literati hear of the Dao,

They laugh heartily at it.

If they did not laugh at it,

It would not be the Dao. ²

Notes:

¹ Lao Zi. *Dao De Jing (Tao-Te Ching)*. Ch.50. See Wang Keping. *The Classic of the Dao: A New Investigation*. (Beijing: Foreign Languages Press, 1998), pp.133-134.

² Ibid., ch.41, p.187.

图书在版编目（CIP）数据

中国人的生存智慧：王柯平 著.
一北京: 外文出版社, 2005 年（2007 重印）
ISBN 978-7-119-04179-7
I. 中... II. 王... III. 人生哲学 - 中国 - 英文
IV. B821

中国版本图书馆CIP数据核字(2005)第 087874 号

特约审读　李　霞
责任编辑　盖中武　杨　璐
版式设计　久品轩工作室
印刷监制　冯　浩

外文出版社网址：
　http://www.flp.com.cn
外文出版社电子信箱：
　info@flp.com.cn
　sales@flp.com.cn

中国人的生存智慧

王柯平 著

© 外文出版社
外文出版社出版
（中国北京百万庄大街 24 号）
邮政编码 100037
三河汇鑫印务有限公司印刷
中国国际图书贸易总公司发行
（中国北京车公庄西路 35 号）
北京邮政信箱第 399 号　邮政编码 100044
2005 年（32 开）第 1 版
2007 年第 1 版第 2 次印刷
（英）
ISBN 　　　　9-7